Celtic Prayers

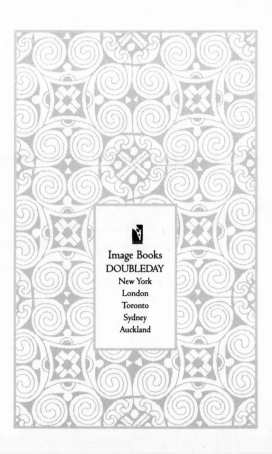

Image Books
DOUBLEDAY
New York
London
Toronto
Sydney
Auckland

CELTIC
PRAYERS

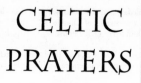

Translated by
Alexander Carmichael

Edited by
Trace Murphy

AN IMAGE BOOK
PUBLISHED BY DOUBLEDAY
a division of
Bantam Doubleday Dell Publishing Group, Inc.
1540 Broadway, New York, New York 10036

Image, Doubleday, and the portrayal of a deer drinking from
a stream are trademarks of Doubleday, a division of Bantam
Doubleday Dell Publishing Group, Inc.

First Image Books edition published March 1996
by special arrangement with Doubleday.

Library of Congress Cataloging-in-Publication Data
Carmina gadelica. English. Selections.
Celtic prayers / translated by Alexander Carmichael:
edited by Trace Murphy. — 1st Image Books ed.
p.   cm.
1. Christian poetry, Gaelic—Translations into English.
2. Incantations, Gaelic—Translations into English.
3. Hymns, Gaelic—Translations into English.
4. Gaelic poetry—Translations into English.
5. Oral tradition—Scotland—Highlands.
6. Oral tradition—Scotland.   7. Prayers.
I. Carmichael, Alexander, 1832–1912.
II. Murphy, Trace.   III. Title.
PB1645.C3213   1996
891.6'31008—dc20   95-46942
CIP

ISBN 0-385-48241-8

Contents

INVOCATIONS

A rune (short poem or incantation) such as this was traditionally used before prayer. At times the speaker would intone it in low, tremulous, unmeasured cadences much like the moving and moaning of the ever murmuring sea on the wild shores of Scotland. This would typically be done in a place of solitude, such as the seashore, where voice can join with the voicing of the waves and praise with the praises of the ceaseless sea.

Rune Before Prayer

I am bending my knee,
In the eye of the Father who created me,
In the eye of the Son who purchased me,
In the eye of the Spirit who cleansed me,
    In friendship and affection.
Through your Anointed One, O God,
Bestow upon us fullness in our need,
        Love towards God,
        The affection of God,
        The smile of God,
        The wisdom of God.
        The grace of God,
        The fear of God,
        And the will of God
To do on the world of the Three,
As angels and saints
Do in heaven;

Each shade and light,
Each day and night,
Each time in kindness,
Give us your Spirit.

A General Supplication

God, listen to my prayer,
Bend to me your ear,
Let my supplications and my prayers
Ascend to you upwards.
Come, King of Glory,
To protect me down,
King of life and mercy
With the aid of the Lamb,
Son of Mary Virgin
To protect me with power,
Son of the lovely Mary
Of purest fairest beauty.

Desires

May I speak each day according to your
    justice,
Each day may I show your chastening, O
    God;
May I speak each day according to your
    wisdom,
Each day and night may I be at peace with
    you.

Each day may I count the causes of your
    mercy,
May I each day give heed to your laws;
Each day may I compose to you a song,
May I harp each day your praise, O God.

May I each day give love to you, Jesu,
Each night may I do the same;
Each day and night, dark and light,
May I laud your goodness to me, O God.

Invocation for Justice

I will go in the name of God,
  In likeness of deer, in likeness of horse,
In likeness of serpent, in likeness of king,
  Stronger am I than all persons.

The hand of God keeping me,
  The love of Christ in my veins,
The strong Spirit bathing me,
  The Three shielding and aiding me,
The Three shielding and aiding me;
  The hand of Spirit bathing me,
The Three each step aiding me.

The Guardian Angel

Angel of God who has charge of me
From the dear Father of mercifulness,
The shepherding kind of the fold of the
    saints
To make round about me this night.

Drive from me every temptation and
    danger,
Surround me on the sea of
    unrighteousness,
And in the narrows, crooks, and straits,
Keep my coracle, keep it always.

Be a bright flame before me,
Be a guiding star above me,
Be a smooth path below me,
And be a kindly shepherd behind me,
Today, tonight, and forever.

I am tired and a stranger,
Lead me to the land of angels;
For me it is time to go home
To the court of Christ, to the peace of
heaven.

Jesu, Thou Son of Mary

Jesu, Son of Mary,
Have mercy upon us,
    Amen.
Jesu, Son of Mary,
Make peace with us,
    Amen.
Oh, with us and for us
Where we shall longest be,
    Amen.
Be about the morning of our course,
Be about the closing of our life,
    Amen.
Be at the dawning of our life,
And oh! at the dark'ning of our day,
    Amen.
Be for us and with us,
Merciful God of all,
    Amen.
Consecrate us

Condition and lot,
King of kings,
God of all,
 Amen.
Consecrate us
Rights and means,
King of kings,
God of all,
 Amen.
Consecrate us
Heart and body,
King of kings,
God of all,
 Amen.
Each heart and body,
Each day to yourself,
Each night accordingly,
King of kings,
God of all,
 Amen.

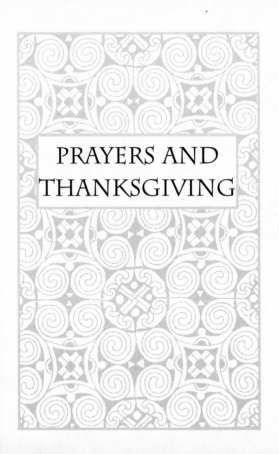

PRAYERS AND THANKSGIVING

As It Was

As it was,
As it is,
As it shall be
Evermore,
O Thou Triune
Of grace!
With the ebb,
With the flow,
O Thou Triune
Of grace!
With the ebb,
With the flow.

Prayer at Dressing

Bless to me, O God,
My soul and my body;
Bless to me, O God,
My belief and my condition;

Bless to me, O God,
My heart and my speech,
And bless to me, O God,
The handling of my hand;

Strength and busyness of morning,
Habit and temper of modesty,
Force and wisdom of thought,
And your own path, O God of virtues,
Till I go to sleep this night;

Your own path, O God of virtues,
Till I go to sleep this night.

My Soul's Healer

My soul's Healer,
Keep me at even,
Keep me at morning,
Keep me at noon,
On rough course faring,
Help and safeguard
My means this night.
I am tired, astray, and stumbling,
Shield me from snare and sin.

A Prayer for Grace

I am bending my knee
In the eye of the Father who created me,
In the eye of the Son who died for me,
In the eye of the Spirit who cleansed me,
    In love and desire.

Pour down upon us from heaven
The rich blessing of your forgiveness;
You who are uppermost in the City,
    Be patient with us.

Grant to us, O Savior of Glory,
The fear of God, the love of God, and his
    affection,
And the will of God to do on earth at all
    times
As angels and saints do in heaven;
Each day and night give us your peace.
    Each day and night give us your peace.

Come I This Day

Come I this day to the Father,
Come I this day to the Son,
Come I to the Holy Spirit powerful;
Come I this day with God,
Come I this day with Christ,
Come I with the Spirit of kindly balm.

God, and Spirit, and Jesus,
From the crown of my head
To the soles of my feet;
Come I with my reputation,
Come I with my testimony,
Come I to you, Jesu;
    Jesu, shelter me.

❧

The Guiding Light of Eternity

O God, who brought me from the rest of
    last night
To the joyous light of this day,
Bring me from the new light of this day
To the guiding light of eternity.
      Oh! from the new light of this day
      To the guiding light of eternity.

❧

Prayer

Thanks to you ever, O gentle Christ,
That you have raised me freely from the
   black
And from the darkness of last night
To the kindly light of this day.

Praise to you, O God of all creatures,
According to each life you have poured on
   me,
My desire, my word, my sense, my repute,
My thought, my deed, my way, my fame.

I Send Witness

I send witness to Mary,
Mother who aids men;
I send witness to Brigit,
Pure tender Nurse of the Lamb;

I send witness to Peter,
Apostle of fear and of sleep;
I send witness to Columba,
Apostle of shore and sea;

I send witness to Heaven,
To the City on the high;
I send witness to Michael,
Noble warrior triumphant;

I send witness to Father,
Who formed all flesh;
I send witness to Christ,
Who suffered scorn and pain;

I send witness to Spirit,
Who will heal my wound,
Who will make me as white
As the cotton grass of the moor.

Hail to You, Mary

Hail to you, Mary, Mother!
You are full of loving grace,
The Lord God is always with you,
Blessed are you, Mary, among women,
Blessed is the fruit of your womb, Jesus,
Blessed are you, Queen of grace;
Holy Mary, Mother of Jesus,
Plead for me a miserable sinner,
Now and at the hour of death,
    Now and at the hour of death.

꘍

Praise of Mary

Flower garland of the ocean,
  Flower garland of the land,
Flower garland of the heavens,
  Mary, Mother of God.

Flower garland of the earth,
  Flower garland of the skies,
Flower garland of the angels,
  Mary, Mother of God.

Flower garland of the mansion,
  Flower garland of the stars,
Flower garland of paradise,
  Mary, Mother of God.

Thoughts

God's will would I do,
My own will bridle;

God's due would I give,
My own due yield;

God's path would I travel,
My own path refuse;

Christ's death would I ponder,
My own death remember;

Christ's agony would I meditate,
My love to God make warmer;

Christ's cross would I carry,
My own cross forget;

Repentance of sin would I make,
Early repentance choose;

A bridle to my tongue I would put,
A bridle on my thoughts I would keep;

God's judgment would I judge,
My own judgment guard;

Christ's redemption would I seize,
My own ransom work;

The love of Christ would I feel,
My own love know.

❧

Encompassment

The holy Apostles' guarding,
The gentle martyrs' guarding,
The nine angels' guarding,
Be cherishing me, be aiding me.

The quiet Brigit's guarding,
The gentle Mary's guarding,
The warrior Michael's guarding,
Be shielding me, be aiding me.

The God of the elements' guarding,
The loving Christ's guarding,
The Holy Spirit's guarding,
Be cherishing me, be aiding me.

Grace Before Food

Be with me, O God, at breaking of bread,
Be with me, O God, at the close of my
    meal;
Let no whit adown my body
That may hurt my sorrowing soul.
    O no whit adown my body
      That may hurt my sorrowing soul.

Thanks After Food

Thanks be to you, O God,
Praise be to you, O God,
Reverence be to you, O God,
For all you have given me.

As you have given life corporeal
To earn me my worldly food,
So grant me life eternal
To show forth your glory.

Grant me grace throughout my life,
Grant me life at the hour of my death;
Be with me, O God, in casting off my
    breath,
O God, be with me in the deep currents.

O! in the parting of the breath,
O! be with my soul in the deep currents.
O God, be with my soul in sounding the
    fords,
In crossing the deep floods.

God's Aid

God to enfold me,
God to surround me,
God in my speaking,
God in my thinking.

God in my sleeping,
God in my waking,
God in my watching,
God in my hoping.

God in my life,
God in my lips,
God in my hands,
God in my heart.

God in my sufficing,
God in my slumber,
God in mine ever living soul,
God in mine eternity.

Birth Baptism

*When a child is born, the midwife puts three small
drops of water on the forehead of the baby while saying:*

The little drop of the Father
On your little forehead, beloved one.

The little drop of the Son
On your little forehead, beloved one.

The little drop of the Spirit
On your little forehead, beloved one.

To aid you from the fays,
To guard you from the host;

To aid you from the gnome,
To shield you from the specter;

To keep you for the Three,
To shield you, to surround you;

To save you for the Three,
To fill you with the graces;

The little drop of the Three,
To lave you with the graces.

*The midwife would then give the child to a nurse to
wash it and the nurse would put a small palmful of
water on the baby while singing:*

A wavelet for your form,
A wavelet for your voice,
A wavelet for your sweet speech;

A wavelet for your luck,
A wavelet for your good,
A wavelet for your health;

A wavelet for your throat,
A wavelet for your pluck,
A wavelet for your graciousness;
Nine waves for your graciousness.

ॐ

Prayer

O God, listen to my prayer,
Let my earnest petition come to you,
for I know that you are hearing me
As surely as though I saw you with mine
   eyes.

I am placing a lock upon my heart,
I am placing a lock upon my thoughts,
I am placing a lock upon my lips
And double-knitting them.

Aught that is amiss for my soul
In the pulsing of my death,
May you, O God, sweep it from me
And may you shield me in the blood of
   your love.

Let no thought come to my heart,
Let no sound come to my ear,
Let no temptation come to my eye,
Let no fragrance come to my nose,

Let no fancy come to my mind,
Let no ruffle come to my spirit,
That is hurtful to my poor body this
    night,
Nor ill for my soul at the hour of my
    death;

But may you yourself, O God of life,
Be at my breast, be at my back,
You to me as a star, you to me as a guide,
From my life's beginning to my life's
    closing.

Thanksgiving

Thanks to you, O God, that I have risen
  today,
To the rising of this life itself;
May it be to your glory, O God of every
  gift,
And to the glory of my soul likewise.

O great God, aid my soul
With the aiding of your own mercy;
Even as I clothe my body with wool,
Cover my soul with the shadow of your
  wing.

Help me to avoid every sin,
And the source of every sin to forsake;
And as the mist scatters on the crest of
  the hills,
May each ill haze clear from my soul, O
  God.

BLESSINGS

This poem, meant to be repeated the first thing on the first day of the year, comes from throughout the Highlands in many different versions.

The Blessing of the New Year

God, bless to me the new day,
Never vouchsafed to me before;
It is to bless your own presence
You have given me this time, O God.

Bless to my eye,
May my eye bless all it sees;
I will bless my neighbor,
May my neighbor bless me.

God, give me a clean heart,
Let me not from sight of your eye;
Bless to me my family,
And bless to me my means.

✥

Blessings

✥

May the Spirit satisfy you
With the water of grace

✥

The blessing of God and the Lord be
    yours,
The blessing of the perfect Spirit be yours,
The blessing of the Three be pouring for
    you
  Mildly and generously,
  Mildly and generously.

✥

The peace of God be to you,
The peace of Christ be to you,
The peace of Spirit be to you,
    And to your children,
    To you and to your children.

※

The eye of the great God be upon you,
The eye of the God of glory be on you,
The eye of the Son of Mary Virgin be on
    you,
The eye of the Spirit mild be on you,
To aid you and to shepherd you;
  Oh the kindly eye of the Three be on
    you,
  To aid you and to shepherd you.

※

    May the everlasting Father Himself
      take you
    In his own generous clasp,
    May God shield you on every steep,
    May Christ keep you in every path,
    May Spirit bathe you in every pass.

※

    May the everlasting Father shield you
    East and west wherever you go.

꙾

May Christ's safeguard protect you ever.

꙾

May God make safe to you each steep,
May God make open to you each pass,
May God make clear to you each road,
And may he take you in the clasp of his
    own two hands.

꙾

Oh may each saint and sainted woman in
    heaven,
O God of the creatures and God of
    goodness,
Be taking charge of you in every strait
Every side and every turn you go.

※

Be each saint in heaven,
Each sainted woman in heaven,
Each angel in heaven
Stretching their arms for you,
Smoothing the way for you,
When you go thither
Over the river hard to see;
    Oh when you go thither home
    Over the river hard to see.

※

May the Father take you
In his fragrant clasp of love,
When you go across the flooding
    streams
And the black river of death.

※

May Mary Virgin's Son himself
Be a generous lamp to you,
To guide you over
The great and awful ocean of eternity.

✙

The compassing of the saints be upon you
The compassing of the angels be upon
    you;
Oh the compassing of all the saints
And of the nine angels be upon you.

✙

The grace of the great God be upon you,
The grace of Virgin Mary's Son be upon
    you,
The grace of the perfect Spirit be upon
    you,
  Mildly and generously.

✙

  May God's blessing be yours,
  And well may it befall you.

✙

  May God's goodness be yours,
  And well and seven times well
  May you spend your lives.

✻

The love of your creator be with you.

✻

May Brigit and Mary and Michael
Shield you on sea and on land,
Each step and each path you travel.

✻

Be the eye of God dwelling with you,
The foot of Christ in guidance with you,
The shower of the Spirit pouring on you,
Richly and generously.
God's peace be to you,
Jesus' peace be to you,
Spirit's peace be to you
And to your children,
Oh to you and to your children,
Each day and night
Of your portion in the world.

꙰

The compassing of the King of life be
    yours,
The compassing of loving Christ be yours,
The compassing of Holy Spirit be yours,
Unto the crown of the life eternal,
    Unto the crown of the life eternal.

꙰

My own blessing be with you,
The blessing of God be with you,
The blessing of Spirit be with you
    And with your children,
With you and with your children.

꙰

My own blessing be with you,
The blessing of God be with you,
The blessing of saints be with you
And the peace of the life eternal,
Unto the peace of the life eternal.

※

The guarding of the God of life be
    on you,
The guarding of loving Christ be on
    you,
The guarding of Holy Spirit be on
    you
Every night of your lives,
    To aid you and enfold you
    Each day and night of your lives.

※

The love and affection of the angels be to
    you,
The love and affection of the saints be to
    you,
The love and affection of heaven be to
    you,
To guard you and to cherish you.
May God shield you on every steep,
May Christ aid you on every path,
May Spirit fill you on every slope,
On hill and on plain.

May the King shield you in the
    valleys,
May Christ aid you on the
    mountains,
May Spirit bathe you on the slopes,
In hollow, on hill, on plain,
Mountain, valley and plain.

❧

The shape of Christ be towards me,
The shape of Christ be to me,
The shape of Christ be before me,
The shape of Christ be behind me,
The shape of Christ be over me,
The shape of Christ be under me,
The shape of Christ be with me,
The shape of Christ be around me
On Monday and on Sunday;
    The shape of Christ be around me
    On Monday and on Sunday.

The love and affection of heaven be to
    you,
The love and affection of the saints be to
    you,
The love and affection of the angels be to
    you,
The love and affection of the sun be to
    you,
The love and affection of the moon be to
    you,
  Each day and night of your lives,
  To keep you from haters, to keep you
    from harmers, to keep you from
    oppressors.

❧

The peace of God be with you,
The peace of Christ be with you,
The peace of Spirit be with you
And with your children,
From the day that we have here today
To the day of the end of your lives.
The grace of God be with you,
The grace of Christ be with you,
The grace of Spirit be with you
And with your children,
For an hour, forever, for eternity.

❧

God's grace distill on you,
Christ's grace distill on you,
Spirit's grace distill on you
Each day and each night
Of your portion in the world;
Oh each day and each night
Of your portion in the world.

※

God's blessing be yours,
And well may it befall you;
Christ's blessing be yours,
And well be you entreated;
Spirit's blessing be yours,
And well spend you your lives,
Each day that you rise up,
Each night that you lie down.

※

May the eye of the great God,
The eye of the God of glory,
The eye of the Virgin's Son,
The eye of the gentle Spirit
Aid you and shepherd you
    In every time,
Pour upon you every hour
    Mildly and generously.

The Celtic Highlanders, being a pastoral people, created a number of prayers and blessings around their pastoral life. "Herding Blessing" is a good example of this and of how a sense of the spiritual was incorporated into the actions of each day.

❧

Herding Blessing

Traveling moorland, traveling townland,
Traveling mossland long and wide,
Be the herding of God the Son about your
    feet,
Safe and whole may you return home,
      Be the herding of God the Son about
        your feet,
      Safe and whole may you return home.

The sanctuary of Carmac and of Columba
Be protecting you going and coming,
And of the milkmaid of the soft palms,
Bride of the clustering hair golden brown,
      And of the milkmaid of the soft
        palms,
      Bride of the clustering hair golden
        brown.

The Mother's Blessing

Where you bring the crown of your head,
Where you bring the tablet of your brow,
Strength be to you therein,
Blessed be to you the powers therein;
Strength be to you therein,
Blessed be to you the powers therein.

Lasting be you in your lying down,
Lasting be you in your rising up,
Lasting be you by night and by day,
And surpassing good be heaven to my dear
    one;
Lasting be you by night and by day,
And surpassing good be heaven to my dear
    one.

The face of God be to your countenance,
The face of Christ the kindly,
The face of the Spirit Holy

Be saving you each hour
In danger and in sorrow;
Be saving you each hour
In danger and in sorrow.

Good Wish

Wisdom of serpent be thine,
Wisdom of raven be thine,
Wisdom of valiant eagle.

Voice of swan be thine,
Voice of honey be thine,
Voice of the Son of the stars.

Bounty of sea be thine,
Bounty of land be thine,
Bounty of the Father of heaven.

Prayer

I pray for you a joyous life,
Honor, estate and good repute,
No sigh from your breast,
No tear from your eye.

No hindrance on your path,
No shadow on your face,
Until you lie down in that mansion,
In the arms of Christ benign.

Grace

Grace of love be yours,
Grace of floor be yours,
Grace of castle be yours,
Grace of court be yours,
Grace and pride of homeland be yours.

The guard of the God of life be yours,
The guard of the loving Christ be yours,
The guard of the Holy Spirit be yours,

> To cherish you,
> To aid you,
> To enfold you.

The Three be about your head,
The Three be about your breast,
The Three be about your body
Each night and each day,
In the encompassment of the Three
Throughout your life long.

❧❧❧

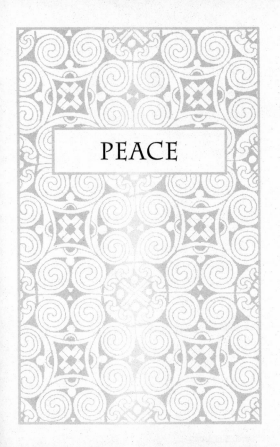

PEACE

Peace

The peace of God, the peace of men,
The peace of Columba kindly,
The peace of Mary mild, the loving,
The peace of Christ, King of tenderness,
   The peace of Christ, King of tenderness.

Be upon each window, upon each door,
Upon each hole that lets in light,
Upon the four corners of my house,
Upon the four corners of my bed,
   Upon the four corners of my bed;

Upon each thing my eye takes in,
Upon each thing my mouth takes in,
Upon my body that is of earth
And upon my soul that came from on
    high,
   Upon my body that is of earth
   And upon my soul that came from on
    high.

Peace

Peace between neighbors,
Peace between kindred,
Peace between lovers,
In love of the King of life.

Peace between person and person,
Peace between wife and husband,
Peace between woman and children,
The peace of Christ above all peace.

Bless, O Christ, my face,
Let my face bless every thing;
Bless, O Christ, mine eye,
Let mine eye bless all it sees.

Peace

The peace of joys,
The peace of lights,
The peace of consolations.

The peace of souls,
The peace of heaven,
The peace of the virgins.

The peace of the fairy bowers,
The peace of peacefulness,
The peace of everlasting.

CREATION

God of the Moon

God of the moon, God of the sun,
God of the globe, God of the stars,
God of the waters, the land, and the skies,
Who ordained to us the King of promise.

It was Mary fair who went upon her knee,
It was the King of life who went upon her
    lap,
Darkness and tears were set behind,
And the star of guidance went up early.

Illumed the land, illumed the world,
Illumed doldrum and current,
Grief was laid and joy was raised,
Music was set up with harp and pedal
    harp.

❧

The Sun

Hail, you sun of the seasons,
As you traverse the skies aloft;
Your steps are strong on the wing of the
    heavens,
You are the glorious mother of the stars.

You lie down in the destructive ocean
Without impairment and without fear;
You rise up on the peaceful wave crest
Like a queenly maiden in bloom.

Queen of the Night

Hail unto thee,
Jewel of the night!

Beauty of the heavens,
Jewel of the night!

Mother of the stars,
Jewel of the night!

Fosterling of the sun,
Jewel of the night!

Majesty of the stars,
Jewel of the night!

New Moon

When I see the new moon,
  It becomes me to lift mine eye,
It becomes me to bend my knee,
  It becomes me to bow my
  head,

Giving thee praise, thou moon of
    guidance,
  That I have seen thee again,
That I have seen the new moon,
  The lovely leader of the way.

Many a one has passed beyond
  In the time between the two
    moons,
Though I am still enjoying earth,
  Thou moon of moons and of
    blessings!

The Golden Butterfly

Butterfly! Butterfly!
Whose soul did you bear,
Butterfly! Butterfly!
Yesterday to heaven?

The Primrose

Primrose, primrose
And wood sorrel,
The children's food
   In summer;
Geimileachd, geimileachd,
Wine and plovers,
The food of men
   In winter.

❧

Omen of the Swans

I heard the sweet voice of the swans,
At the parting of night and day,
Gurgling on the wings of traveling,
   Pouring forth their strength on high.

I quickly stood me, nor made I move,
A look which I gave forth to see
Who should be guiding in front?
   The queen of fortune, the white swan.

This was on the evening of Friday,
My thoughts were of the Tuesday:
I lost my means and my kinsfolk,
   A year from that Friday, forever.

Should you see a swan of Friday,
In the joyous morning dawn,
There shall be increase on your means and
     kin,
   Nor shall your flocks be always dying.

The brisgein *(root of the silverweed)* is often mentioned in the old songs and sayings, for it was much used by the people. Before the potato was introduced, this root was cultivated as part of the basic diet and considered palatable and nutritious. The brisgein *was either boiled,* roasted, or sometimes dried and ground into meal for bread and porridge.

Silverweed

Honey underground
Silverweed of spring.
Honey and condiment
Whisked whey of summer.
Honey and fruitage
Carrot of autumn.
Honey and crunching
Nuts of winter
Between Feast of Andrew
   And Christmastide.

The Shamrock

Shamrock of foliage,
    Shamrock of entwining,
Shamrock of the prayer,
    Shamrock of my love.

Shamrock of my sorrow,
    Plant of Patrick of the virtues,
Shamrock of the Son of Mary,
    Journey's end of the peoples.

Shamrock of grace,
    Of joy, of the tombs,
It were my wish in death
    You should grow on my grave.

ऊँ ऊँ ऊँ

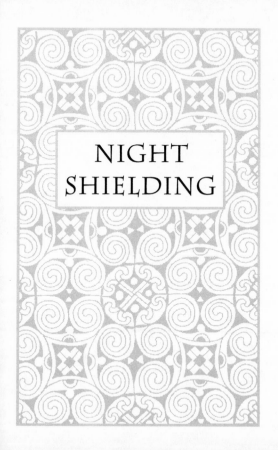

NIGHT
SHIELDING

Bless, O God, the Dwelling

Bless, O God, the dwelling,
And each who rests herein this night;
Bless, O God, my dear ones
In every place wherein they sleep;

In the night that is tonight,
And every single night;
In the day that is today,
And every single day.

This rune is to be said by travelers at night for protection from all harm on their journey.

Charm for Fear by Night

God before me, God behind me,
God above me, God below me;
I on the path of God,
   God upon my track.

Who is there on land?
Who is there on wave?
Who is there on billow?
Who is there by doorpost?
Who is along with us?
   God and Lord.

I am here abroad,
I am here in need,
I am here in pain,
I am here in straits,
I am here alone,
   O God, aid me.

Repose of Sleep

O God of life, darken not to me your
  light,
O God of life, close not to me your joy,
O God of life, shut not to me your door,
O God of life, refuse not to me your
  mercy,
O God of life, quench to me your wrath,
And O God of life, crown to me your
  gladness,
O God of life, crown to me your gladness.